Body   er

INSTITUTE OF LEADERSHIP & MANAGEMENT (ILM)
THE PROFESSIONAL INSTITUTE OF CHOICE FOR TODAY'S MANAGER

Founded over 50 years ago and now part of the City & Guilds Group, the Institute of Leadership & Management (ILM) is unique among professional bodies. As the largest awarding body for management-related qualifications with over 75,000 candidates each year, the ILM recognises and fosters good management practice. As a professional body, ILM also offers informal personal and professional support to practising leaders and managers across all disciplines and at every career stage.

20,000 members have already found that ILM membership gives them the strategic, ongoing support they need to fulfil their aims, enabling them to enhance their skills, add to their professional expertise and to develop a wider network of valuable business contacts.

For further information on becoming a member of ILM please contact the Membership Department on telephone + 44 (0) 1543 251 346. www.i-l-m.com

Body Language and the First Line Manager

EUNICE LAWTON

Chandos Publishing
Oxford · England

Published in association with

Institute of Leadership
& Management

Chandos Publishing (Oxford) Limited
Chandos House
5 & 6 Steadys Lane
Stanton Harcourt
Oxford OX29 5RL
UK
Tel: +44 (0) 1865 884447 Fax: +44 (0) 1865 884448
Email: info@chandospublishing.com
www.chandospublishing.com

First published in Great Britain in 2006

ISBN:
1 84334 215 4 (paperback)
1 84334 216 2 (hardback)
978 1 84334 215 1 (paperback)
978 1 84334 216 8 (hardback)

© E. Lawton, 2006

British Library Cataloguing-in-Publication Data.
A catalogue record for this book is available from the British Library.

Typeset by Domex e-Data Pvt. Ltd.
Printed in the UK and USA.

Contents

Preface

As a manager and a trainer I have all too often seen staff struggle with the transition from worker to supervisor. Numerous students have recounted their ordeals which have involved pain, confusion and even resignation. Suddenly the world has changed and no one warned them that things will never be the same again. The afterglow of promotion can soon fade into feelings of loneliness and being unable to cope.

This book has been written with the aim of helping supervisors adjust to their new role by providing advice on how they can improve the way they communicate in all the different situations that they now face. This information has been provided to help make the transition less painful and hopefully improve the way they initially cope and thereby improve their chances of being successful.

About the author

Eunice Lawton is Yorkshire born, living in a village on the outskirts of Sheffield with her husband Keith of 23 years and their two children, Daniel and Maria.

Eunice is an experienced manager and trainer, having worked in the public, private and voluntary sector and currently provides management development training through collages and other training providers.

In her spare time she enjoys playing the piano and listening to her husband play in a local brass band. She enjoys village life and takes part in local pub quizzes and other events, in addition to being a member of the local leisure centre.

The author may be contacted via the publishers.

Body language and the first line manager

Introduction

The change from being simply one of the team, to being the supervisor or first line manager, is often one of the biggest changes that will take place in someone's working life. Others will frequently gain the impression that such a move changes the person, but usually the first thing to change is the attitudes of those around them. Suddenly everything they do is noticed and everything they say is analysed by their staff. The staff will also test the boundaries of a new supervisor even if it is someone they have previously worked with. All this takes place when someone is new to the role and new to supervising staff, thereby doubling the pressure.

Eventually the new supervisor will make changes to the way they behave, to respond to the new situation they find themselves in. They may learn the hard way, that they need to choose their words more carefully and take more time to make decisions, to ensure they can stand up to scrutiny, as staff start to question their reasoning. It is impossible to carry on as before, as the relationship with former work colleagues is now on a different basis. This can often lead to the end of friendships either because of jealousy or because to continue such a friendship becomes unworkable. No one said being a manager would be easy.

The change in role is difficult enough as instead of doing the work, the new manager is now responsible for the work being done through others. The tasks now being carried out differ substantially from work previously undertaken, as the new manager is now responsible for managing budgets, appraising staff, attending business meetings, monitoring performance and allocating work. If they are lucky they will have had some practice at some of these when filling in temporarily for the previous supervisor during absence or sickness, but it is surprising how many people make this move with little or no experience. Even for those who have had some practice, the realisation that there is no longer someone above you, that you can refer to, and that you have to cope on your own, can be quite daunting.

Management mostly involves interacting with other people, and therefore the way you communicate is crucial to your success. The aim of this book is to provide a starting point on assessing your own image and the way you communicate so that if you aspire, or have recently moved into such a position, you will be provided with the basic information to help you decide on how you can improve your non-verbal communication and therefore greatly increase your chances of success as a manager.

The importance of non-verbal communication

Our non-verbal communication or body language plays a vital part in how we communicate at work and yet this is something that is usually given little thought.

It can make the difference between success and failure. If we communicate badly it can have a detrimental effect on our performance.

It is estimated that over 70 per cent of our communication is non-verbal. This covers a wide range of areas, such as the clothes you wear, your posture, the rate at which you speak, facial expressions and how you position yourself in relation to others. Some examples of these are now quite widely known, such as:

- your pupils get bigger when you see someone you like;
- crossing your arms suggests you are defensive or feeling negative;
- when people copy your body language they agree with you.

Awareness of body language helps you to find out whether you are being understood, by observing how other people react to you, and consequently realise the impact that you are having on them. Body language is natural and normal but its importance is often underestimated or even ignored. People who are skilled in body language look for the signs that will help them to interpret the non-verbal signals of others. They also know how to give the right impression by the body language they use, deliberately using it to make the desired impact on other people.

From childhood we are taught to hide our thoughts and feelings so that we can become polite members of society. We are encouraged to hide our disappointments and not to show our dislike of people. This means that as adults we naturally try to hide our thoughts and feelings, and do not say or show what we really think or feel. We may think we are concealing our thoughts and emotions but usually our body language gives us away.

There are two main reasons why understanding body language can be useful:

- As you become more aware of your own body language you can make changes to ensure you are more effective in your communication. By giving attention to your body language you can ensure that you provide the right impression to others, for example, understanding, sympathy, trust, knowledge, respect.

- You can improve the way you read the body language of others so that you can gain a better understanding of them. By being aware of the response of others you will be able to assess how well you are being understood and what their reactions may mean.

As a leader and manager, the people around you will be looking for you to display the desired type of behaviour. By controlling what you say with your own body language, you can ensure you make a positive and lasting impression. The more aware you become of your own body language, the more easily you will recognise the non-verbal clues given out by other people. By giving thought to your own body language, and that of others, you can improve the way you perform at work in the many varied situations you face as a manager, for example, briefing staff, making presentations, welcoming clients, negotiating deals.

In these and many other situations you can begin to feel more confident and in control, as you improve the ways in which you interact with others and thereby increase your chances of being successful.

First impressions

In the world of business, the first impression you make can be the difference between success and failure. This is vital in many situations you will face, such as internal and external interviews, meetings with groups of staff, presenting your ideas, attending business meetings and managing customer relationships.

It is important to be in control of your body language to ensure you always make the best possible impression on others. The way you dress, your choice of style and your posture will all give out messages to others about the way you view yourself and the way you wish to be viewed.

When we first meet people, we briefly look at their overall image before focusing on their face. The first thing we usually notice is the clothes they are wearing. From this, we make assumptions about them in terms of their personality, status and many others areas. If you are not happy with your current image, then you need to consider making changes as your image will influence the way people will perceive you. Making changes can also improve how you view yourself and increase your self-confidence.

Even if you are generally happy with yourself, it is a good idea to occasionally review your image to see if there is room for improvement. This will ensure you have not let things slip and are keeping up to date with current trends, where necessary, or just giving yourself a lift by trying something different. This can show that you are adaptable and capable of moving with the times.

To review your appearance you need to study yourself and decide what needs to be improved. A good place to start is with your clothes. Go through your work clothes and decide what is in a good state of repair and suits the image you want to make and throw away anything that is past its best or does not match the look you are aiming for. You may need to seek professional help to find out the style and colours that suit you. Some department stores offer this service for free and it is well worth a visit as they can often provide you with valuable advice. You can observe others to gain ideas on what may look good on you and what the current fashions are. You may need to invest in some new items, in which case buy the best you can afford and seek to coordinate clothes so that you can obtain the maximum wear out of each item.

You could try a new hairstyle – a new look can boost your confidence and give you a more business-like image. Many hairstylists will be able to give you advice on what may suit you. If you are not happy with your weight, you could try to find out which diet and method of exercise suits your lifestyle. You should obtain medical advice to find out what is appropriate and safe for you. There are many sources of advice available which provide details on how you can improve your body, skin etc.

Once you have decided on the changes you need to make, be realistic about what can be achieved and, if necessary, introduce the changes gradually. By improving your image you can ensure you make a positive and lasting impression on everyone you meet.

Your image at work

To succeed in management you need to ensure that you not only look good, but have a good image at work, and this should be worked on constantly.

Here a few areas you could consider:

■ *Posture*: You should aim to sit and stand in a positive manner. Avoid any kind of stooping which may come across as apologetic or unsure. If you lean forward when you are communicating with others this can look dominating and therefore intimidating to some people. Leaning to one side can imply a hidden agenda, lack of conviction or uncertainty. You should aim for an upright, balanced posture which shows that you are confident in what you are saying without intimidating others.

- *Desks*: As managers aim to get work done though others, a cluttered desk gives out many negative messages, such as being unorganised, unable to delegate, bad at time management and having confused thinking. Aim to keep your workspace clean and tidy so that you look in control of the situation and have the time to respond to situations as required.

- *Dress*: Clothes can be used to influence how others will view your status. Some colours can imply power, for example, navy, red and black. Your clothing should always fit and hang well. A tailored suit will always make you look high profile. Your outfit should be appropriate to the situation, so be aware of the dress code in your organisation and that of others when visiting elsewhere. Pay attention to detail and make sure footwear is well maintained and accessories coordinated.

- *Walk the walk*: Walk around in a confident manner and avoid rushing by setting off in good time for any appointments. Avoid carrying too many items as this can make you look overloaded and unable to cope. It can also prevent you being able to interact with others, for example, by shaking hands. The aim should be to glide along with a positive gaze and give the impression that you know where you are going.

- *Interacting with others*: Practise giving a firm handshake, which should not crush the knuckles of the other person or appear too limp. Try to use people's names where possible, as this will always impress them and build a bond between you, but do not overdo this to the point where it appears false. Show interest in people when they are talking to you, by facing them and making eye contact. Aim to be calm as this always looks confident.

- *Avoid nervous displays*: Do not fidget with your hands as this makes you appear nervous or untrustworthy. If you are in an office or at a meeting, keep nervous fidgeting under control by clasping your hands on top of a desk or table, or behind your back while standing.

- *Answering questions*: If you are unsure of an answer, do not start to stare at the ceiling or out of the window. Keep eye contact with the person and maintain a steady gaze. This may even encourage them to say something further and, at the very least, will make you seem confident and thoughtful, rather than desperate. If you do not know the answer, offer to find out or redirect them to someone who will know, rather than trying to make up an answer and getting caught out.

- *Asking for help*: Always be positive when you need to ask for help. Try to look more confident than you actually feel. When you are in a new role or situation you cannot be expected to know everything, so there is no need to look worried or apologetic. If you make notes when others are providing you with advice or information, this will then make you appear to be well organised, willing to learn and taking your responsibilities seriously.

- *Dealing with time wasters*: If some people take up too much of your time, stand up when they come to see you, and do not offer them a seat. If necessary, start to walk out of the room towards a general area while finding out what they want. Without appearing rude, you need to avoid letting people take up too much of your time. You can achieve this by sending out subconscious messages via your body language.

- *Positive listening*: Give people your full attention when they are speaking to you and use positive listening skills to demonstrate that they have your full attention. This includes maintaining eye contact, matching their facial expressions and not trying to interrupt. In the fast pace of today's business life, we often start multi-tasking to make the best use of our time; however, if you carry on reading and replying to emails and the like while someone needs your attention, it will give the impression that they are unimportant to you and that you are not really listening to what they have to say. This will damage your relationship with that person.

- *Over-responding*: In our attempt to get on with people it is easy to appear too interested and too enthusiastic during everyday conversations. If you appear to be 'over the top', you will come across as insincere and people may start to distrust you as a result. Make sure your responses are always appropriate to the situation.

- *Responding to mistakes*: If you make a mistake, try to minimise the effect by keeping your body still and your facial expression calm. You need to avoid drawing attention to yourself or the situation. Apologise once but do not keep on saying sorry. Do not explain further unless you are required to do so. This way mistakes can be overcome and soon forgotten as there is no drama involved.

Achieving assertiveness

There are a variety of people in organisations who come across in a non-assertive way, who end up feeling that work is not as fulfilling as it could be, and who are held back from career progression because of their lack of assertiveness. These are the people who are either too passive or aggressive in their manner and as a result will keep missing out on opportunities as they end up being either overlooked or avoided.

The aim should be to come across as an assertive person, which means coming across in a balanced way that is neither aggressive or passive. Assertiveness means considering ourselves and others so that we act in a fair way which benefits both sides. This is different from being aggressive, where we are only interested in getting our own way, or passive where we give in to others to our own detriment.

Being assertive involves the use of body language to support the words we use, otherwise we undermine what we are trying to achieve. Our non-verbal communication will show our true stance, and may be seen in the examples in Table 1.

You need to be assertive at all times, not just when you think there will be a conflict situation. By practising assertiveness in everyday situations you will build up your confidence and be

Table 1   Body language and behaviour

	Passive	Assertive	Aggressive
Voice	Too soft, trembling and monotone, nervous laugh, sighing	A steady voice with a varied tone to support what is being said	Too loud, sharp and snappy
Body	Arms crossed, drooped shoulders fidgeting, leaning slightly away, nervous movements	Open gestures with no barriers made, evenly balanced posture with arms or legs, steady movements	Very erect with chest stuck out and leaning forward, uses pointed finger, interrupting gestures
Face	Over-smiling or false smile, features change rapidly	A smile that reaches the eyes, steady and relaxed features	Scowls, raised eyebrows, jutted jaw
Eye contact	Reduced with more evasive or downward glances	Even gaze without staring and used when listening and speaking	Staring and dominating

more assertive when more difficult situations arise. By demonstrating your assertiveness in less threatening situations you will send out the signals that say that you are not willing to be put upon, which, in turn, can lead to people being less likely to try to take advantage of you.

Raising your profile

Once you have worked on your overall image, the next step is to raise your profile so that your image is extended beyond your immediate place of work. Raising your profile will gain you a wider range of contacts that will help you to succeed in your current role and become more aware of future opportunities.

The image you present can make a big difference to how you perform in many situations. Managers with a high profile are the ones who will be offered opportunities and promotions rather than those who just do a good job and hide their talents. In many job interviews, it is those with good interview skills who are successful rather than those who are the most suitable for the position.

Business requires you to use a different kind of body language to that in your home or social life. Body language can give things away, so this must be controlled as much as possible, usually by keeping facial expressions and head movements to a minimum. Powerful people tend to use less movement than others, as they do not feel they have to attract attention by their gestures, they just expect people to take notice of them and listen to what they have to say.

When making eye contact in business, you should look at the area around the eyes and bridge of the nose. If you look higher, you may appear arrogant, while looking lower down at the mouth area can make people uncomfortable, as this is considered to be a more intimate gaze. Eye contact needs to be steady without actually staring, which is seen as threatening or rude.

Listening is an important skill in business. Many people fail to listen properly, so colleagues and clients are impressed by anyone who takes the trouble to listen to them. Show you are listening by giving eye contact, leaning forward, nodding and mirroring their facial expression.

The following are suggestions on how to improve your profile:

- Demonstrate good manners by being charming and polite at all times. Do not become involved in gossiping about others or complaining about your place of work.

- Take the time to visit other members of staff and ask them about current work issues. Use good listening skills to show concern. This helps you to keep in touch with what is going on, increases your range of contacts, thus creating the image of being a good manager.

- If you attend any work social event, avoid drinking too much so that you do not ruin the image you have worked hard to build. If necessary, leave early if the event seems to be getting out of hand.

- Networking outside your own area of the organisation is a good way of finding out about the business as a whole and developing a wide range of contacts. This will increase your background knowledge so that you generally come across as more knowledgeable, adding to your image as someone who keeps up-to-date. Attend network meetings, seminars and conferences that will provide you with the updated knowledge you need and the opportunity to mix with other people that you can then contact afterwards to discuss ideas, developments etc.

- Find a mentor, even if there is no official mentoring programme available. You can ask a senior manager who has the kind of experience and connections that will be helpful to your development. Most people are flattered by being asked and enjoy giving others the benefit of their experience, so do not be afraid to ask.

- Look for role models in your organisation. Are there any high-flyers who you could benefit from by observing and finding out what made them successful?

- Be open to opportunities that will give you the opportunity to shine by taking part in any projects or secondments that will help you to be more widely known or operate at a higher level.

Body language basics

Not everyone shares the same body language as this can vary depending upon their upbringing, experiences and culture. There is no precise definition of gestures and therefore body language needs to be interpreted within context. Any information provided is only a general guide as there can be wide variations.

When reading the body language of other people it is important to observe them over a period of time, where possible, to become familiar with how they normally express themselves. Interpreting someone's thoughts and feelings based on a single example will result in errors, as each action can have several different meanings. It is only by observing several actions, which suggest a similar meaning, that an accurate conclusion can be made.

This means observing the body as a whole rather than just relying on facial expressions, which is where our gaze tends to focus. Observe their posture and limb movements to look for other signals that support any head and face movements to give a clearer indication of what is really going on. Is their overall non-verbal communication open or closed throughout their body? Do not underestimate your instincts – you may subconsciously pick up on things which give you a certain impression; look for body language to back this up.

As with learning any new skill, you may initially find it difficult to interpret non-verbal communication. It will require practice to develop this skill; start by taking the time to become more aware of your own behaviour on a daily basis. If you can recognise your own responses, and become more familiar with what these mean to you, then it will help you to better understand the responses of others. Try to be aware of single clues at first, then build up to looking for groups of clues that provide an overall and more accurate meaning.

Body movement

People are aware that others mostly look at their faces when communicating, so they try to keep their facial expressions under control. This often means they do not pay as much attention to the rest of their body, so it is here that the real clues are provided.

Our bodies generally show either a closed or open position. Closed positions present a negative stance, with the body made to appear smaller by keeping the extremities close together. For example, arms and legs may be crossed to form a barrier.

Open positions show a positive stance with the head held high, arms outstretched with palms showing and legs stood comfortably apart.

If we do not feel comfortable with someone, we normally take up a closed body position. This can happen when we do not know someone well or have met them for the first time.

In these situations, we naturally feel vulnerable and want to protect ourselves; this is reflected in our body position. As we develop a relationship, we become more open and our body language changes to reflect this.

Turning towards or away

When we turn our body towards people, we are signalling that we are interested in what they have to say or we are showing respect for them. If the other person turns to face us, then they are returning our interest and showing acceptance of us. If we turn away we are showing that we are no longer interested and are just waiting until we can get away, as we would rather be somewhere else.

Out of politeness people will often face you and smile and nod while talking but their body and feet will show if they are really interested. If the body and feet are pointing towards you then they are comfortable with the situation. If their body and feet are pointing away from you, then they are feeling uncomfortable and want to get away.

The more we like and agree with people, the closer we move our body to them. If others start to move their body away from us, this is a sign that they disagree or are uncertain. If they move from side to side or back and forth, then this can show doubt or insecurity.

Head

By observing someone's head movements we can usually tell if they agree or disagree with us, as the 'yes' and 'no' gestures are subconscious and usually take place without their being aware of it. The gesture will usually be slight, and can be accompanied by matching eye movement as they briefly look down as they move their head sideways or maintain eye contact while nodding.

In most countries, the nodding gesture is a positive one which suggests agreement and interest, with the shaking head used to express disagreement. This is not always the case with some cultures, indeed, sometimes these gestures are used the opposite way around. You should check up on this when travelling abroad or hosting visitors from another country.

The nodding gesture can also be used in other ways, such as trying to gain approval from others. It can therefore be seen as more powerful to keep your head movements to a minimum. Nodding too much can mean that someone wants to interrupt as they have heard enough; it signals that they feel they understand what you are saying and want to add to it or put across their own view. This is usually accompanied by other signals from the hands or eyes.

Tilting the head at an angle can show an interest in what is being said but can also indicate they are suspicious or uncertain, so you need to look for other signals to help you interpret the situation. Turning the head slightly can mean they are trying to hear you better so they can evaluate what is being said.

Rubbing the back of the head or neck is a sign that they have heard enough and are no longer interested in what is being said.

Posture

The way a person stands presents significant insight into their feelings. It is often one of the first things we notice and it can provide us with much recognisable information, such as positive or negative attitudes when people look interested or bored, confident or nervous.

We can tell straight away if someone is feeling down, as they hang their head and avoid eye contact. They are not interested in anyone or anything except their own misery. They walk more slowly, slightly bent over with slumped shoulders, as if they are bearing the weight of their unhappiness. Their facial expression will be unsmiling and grim.

When someone is happy they display the opposite by holding their head up and having an upright body. They look around, showing interest in their surroundings and making eye contact with people. They walk briskly and with purpose.

Posture can indicate how you will respond to a request. When you are asked to do something, if your posture is upright with open arms, you indicate that you are willing to take on the task; however, if you are standing in a slumped position with arms folded, then you will appear unwilling to be involved.

A rigid body posture shows anxiety and nervousness. Tension causes the shoulders to move upwards and closer together. The shoulders fall when people are disappointed or deflated. Shrugging the shoulders can also communicate a lack of conviction in what is being said or listened to.

The hands-on-hip position is usually interpreted as being aggressive. The position expands the body to take up more room and as a result makes it look confrontational.

Arms

Arms are used as part of the open and closed body positions. As they are usually more likely to be visible above the level of a desk or table, we can interpret their movements when we cannot see the lower half of the body.

The open arms position signifies that someone is in a positive frame of mind. If these change to become folded, then we know the situation has changed and that the person is no longer in agreement with what is being said.

If someone moves away and puts their arm over the back of the chair then this turning away shows a negative response. This can indicate the need to gain more space due to feeling threatened and needing to establish their position.

Arms crossed high on the chest is a closed position and can mean several things:

- they are showing they do not like the person who is communicating with them;

- the arms are used as a barrier when someone feels they are under attack;

- they are physically trying to stop the communication coming through as they disagree or do not find it relevant to themselves.

If you feel the crossed arms show disagreement, then this gives you the opportunity to find out why. In this way you can deal with any queries or concerns that are blocking your message getting through. If they seem to be hugging themselves with the crossed arms, this could indicate their need to be reassured.

If you can get people to uncross their arms this will unconsciously help them to change their negative attitude and improve your chances of persuading them to understand your position. You can try and get them to uncross their arms by asking them to do something, such as holding something or passing something around. You can also try getting them to mirror you by folding your arms and then unfolding them to see if they will follow.

Hands

There are many hand gestures used throughout the world which can have different meanings in different countries. The hands need to be interpreted with other signals as they may not give you the full picture on their own. We move our hands around without giving consideration to what they reveal.

Hands can be steepled to show superiority. This is often used in certain professions where it is used to convey a superior position or knowledge in relation to the other person, for example, the teacher/student or the doctor/patient. The steepled hands are usually raised while they are talking and lowered while they are listening.

Palm gripping behind the back is a confident position. This is a sign they are not afraid of anything as it leaves their front exposed and vulnerable to attack. By adopting this position you can appear confident and in control. If the hands are clasped behind the head instead of the back, this also shows a dominant or superior position.

Open palms are generally considered a positive non-verbal message. This goes back to medieval days when open palms indicated that a person had no weapons. Today they generally indicate that a person has nothing to hide.

Negative hand movements include:

- hand wringing can show worry or a lack of self-confidence;
- fidgeting takes place when people are nervous or worried;
- playing with pens by doodling or drumming is a sign of inattention due to boredom;
- tapping fingers indicates agitation, anxiety and boredom;

- hands in pockets can indicate feelings of uncertainty and suspicion;
- touching areas of the face or clothing suggests nervousness.

Legs and feet

The legs and feet are the furthest away from the brain and as a result can be hard to control. If they are hidden beneath desks and tables it is less easy to gather clues from them. Think how vulnerable you feel when you have to sit on a chair in front of a panel of people with your legs and feet on view. You will feel under pressure as you need to control all of your body movements and do not have the security of partly hiding behind something.

If you want to appear to be open and honest then do not cross your legs. By keeping your legs uncrossed, your feet flat on the floor and slightly leaning forward you send out a message of being open and cooperative. You can show that you are focusing on people by pointing your body and feet in their direction.

People can often appear to be very confident and in control in the top half of their body, but give themselves away by using negative leg and foot movements, showing nervousness or uncertainty. Examples of these movements would be:

- frequently shifting their leg positions;
- having the legs crossed with one of them bouncing on the other;
- rocking back and forth on their heels;
- the legs crossed away, presenting a barrier;
- foot-tapping, showing that they are impatient.

Facial displays

The human face is more highly developed than any other animal when it comes to expression; indeed, there are 80 muscles in the face that can be used to express our many moods. There are thought to be six main of facial expressions that are common throughout the world:

- happy;
- disgusted;
- frightened;
- angry;
- surprised;
- sad.

The frequency of facial movements increases when people are trying to be persuasive. It seems, also, that different parts of the face give clues to different emotions. For example, fear is clearest in the eyes, while anger manifests in the lower face, brows and forehead.

People touch their face when they are nervous. Touching the area around the mouth can be a sign of lying or thinking that the other person is lying.

A single raised eyebrow can mean surprise or concern.

Eye movement

How you make eye contact is very important when interacting with others as it can be used in either a positive or negative manner. If we cannot see someone's eyes, for example, if they are wearing sunglasses, we find this unsettling as without being able to look into someone's eyes, we are never sure of their intentions and cannot judge their reactions. Eye contact forms a major part of non-verbal communication.

How we gaze at people's faces can also have different meaning and effect on them. It is thought that we generally look at people around the eyes and nose area; this is seen as friendly and is usually acceptable. If we are not happy with people, or want to be dominant, then the gaze will rise to just above the eyes to give a feeling of superiority. This can also make us appear to be very serious. As people become more intimate with each other the gaze will drop down to include the mouth area. If this happens inappropriately then it can cause discomfort.

Positive contact

Just looking at someone can signal that we are interested in them and willing to talk to them. When we start to talk to someone, we maintain eye contact to show our interest in them and gain rapport. The more eye contact there is, the more likely there is to be a positive response.

During conversations we use eye contact to give out signals about when we want to say something or when we are expecting someone else to say something. A continued gaze will encourage others to keep speaking as they think we are interested in what they have to say.

Our pupils dilate if we see someone we find attractive. The large pupils will make us appear more childlike and therefore more appealing to another person.

Negative contact

If we are not interested in someone, or their conversation, we avoid making eye contact to show this. Failing to maintain eye contact gives the impression that we are no longer interested and would rather be elsewhere.

Random eye movement that keeps changing direction suggests that someone is nervous and is looking for a means of escape from an uncomfortable situation.

If people are talking to us and they fail to make eye contact, we get the impression that they are being insincere, dishonest or holding something back.

Too much eye contact, however, can be negative as staring can make people feel uncomfortable. Staring can be seen as aggressive and lead to conflict if it is interpreted in this way.

Withdrawing eye contact by lowering the eyes is usually taken as a means of submission or shyness.

Eye direction

There has been much research into how the eyes look towards the part of the brain that is being accessed at any one time. It is thought that this gives us an indication as to how a person is thinking.

The left side of the brain is the factual and analytical side, while the right side of the brain deals with our more creative thoughts. On this basis, if we move our eyes up and to the right we are accessing the left side of the brain and probably telling the truth. If we look up and to the left we are accessing the right side and therefore it is likely that we are making things up.

You can test this out by asking people questions to which you know the answers. You can then be fairly certain of the meaning of such eye movements. There are some people who may operate the other way around, just as some people are left-handed, so it is better to check before making assumptions.

Voice

We use our voice to give expression to our words in an effort to provide greater clarity to our communication. The written word does not have this facility, and this is why misunderstandings can occur when we use letters or e-mails as our chosen method of communicating. How many times have you received a written message and pondered over the intention behind the words and as a result needed to contact the person for clarification? When speaking, our emphasis of one particular word can change the meaning of a sentence. For example, 'I did not say you stole the wallet' can change meaning if the italicised word is emphasised:

- '*I* did not say you stole the wallet' – someone else said it.

- 'I did not say *you* stole the wallet' – I said someone else did.

- 'I did not say *stole* the wallet' – I said you moved it.

- 'I did not say you stole the *wallet*' – I said you stole the car keys.

Our non-verbal communication can override the actual spoken word. This is why the children's game 'Simon Says' catches people out. We follow a person's actions rather than their verbal commands. You can test this by asking someone to carry out an action and at the same time demonstrate a different one. For example, try pointing in one direction and telling someone to go the opposite way. All too often they will copy your actions and ignore your words as they will assume you must mean the demonstrated action, at the very least, they will ask for clarification as you will have confused them.

You may wish to give consideration to certain areas in the way you use your voice, such as:

- *Speed*: We can create empathy by matching the rate of speech of another person. Generally, you need to consider whether you talk too fast or too slow as these can both have negative effect on your communication. Too fast can make you sound nervous or hurried, while too slow can make you sound uninterested. We use the speed of our voice to show urgency by increasing our speed; to emphasise something we speak more slowly and deliberately.

- *Volume*: By speaking too loudly we can come across as intimidating; too soft can make us sound nervous and shy.

- *Pitch*: This refers to the way our voice will rise and fall while speaking or even the way it drones by staying at the same level. Most people naturally keep changing their pitch as they speak to emphasise certain points and to keep people's attention.

- *Ending a sentence*: When asking a question, we normally raise the pitch at the end. If we do this with a statement rather than a question, it makes us sound uncertain. When making a statement, the pitch should stay the same throughout. We come across as commanding if the pitch goes down at the end. So, if you wish to be taken seriously, try to make your pitch go down at the end of your sentences.

- *Emotion*: Our voice will give an indication of our emotions, for example:

  - *very loud, rapid speech*: anger or wanting to override the other person's opinion;

  - *slow speech with a low pitch and volume*: boredom or lack of interest;

  - *irregular speech and breathing*: alarm or excitement.

  Sometimes we deliberately show emotion in our voice as that is how we want to interpreted. We often want people to know if we are pleased or upset so will use the appropriate pitch, level and speed to show this.

Silence

Even when we are silent we can be communicating various different attitudes. Silence can be used in many ways and can have different meanings:

- *Showing respect*: We will keep quiet and let others speak out of respect if they are more senior or more knowledgeable than ourselves.

- *Encouraging others to speak*: Keeping quiet when someone has finished speaking will often encourage them to continue speaking and provide you with more information.

- *Showing disapproval*: If someone refuses to speak or does not speak when expected, this can signal disapproval of the person or what is being said.

- *Showing interest*: If we are listening and being silent, then we show interest in what is being said and will accompany this by:

  - making verbal affirmations, such as 'A-ha ' 'Mmm';

  - keep changing our facial movements to match the speaker;

  - smiling and nodding slowly.

  This will often encourage them to talk for longer.

- *Comfortable silences*: When we do not know people well, a period of silence can become embarrassing with both parties trying to think of something to say to fill the void. When we are familiar with people, silences are no longer uncomfortable as you can relax and speak when you want.

- *Reflective silence*: If the subject is complex or emotive then people will need time to reflect; silences occur to help this process. You should allow people the space to think by not interrupting the silence when this takes place.

Time

Timing can be used to demonstrate our control of situations, what we think of other people or how we view our importance compared with others.

By keeping people waiting we are showing how our time is more valuable than theirs and that we are more important. We are showing that we expect them to be prepared to wait for our availability. By arriving late for group meetings we are again showing that we consider ourselves to be too busy to turn up on time and that we expect people to wait for us. This can be a sign of disrespect to others. It can also be used to intimidate people if they are already in stressful situation, such as waiting for an interview or a disciplinary meeting.

The time allowed for interacting with people needs to be appropriate to the situation and this needs to be considered when booking meetings. The length of time that we allow people gives them an impression of how much they are valued. If we allow sufficient time for people, we show that we consider them to be of value. This is important when meeting with staff for appraisals. If insufficient time is allowed then we are giving staff the impression they do not deserve our time and they are of little importance. Cutting meetings short can give a negative message and appear to be disrespectful.

Environment

Our environment will send out messages about ourselves to others. Others will gain an impression of us by the way we set up our workspace and by what we choose to display in it.

We do not often have much choice over the furniture we inherit in our work space, but we do have some leeway in how it is arranged. Does your desk form a barrier between you and anyone who walks through the door? Do you sit with your back to the window so that you look as if a divine light radiates from you? Is everything piled up on the floor as if you cannot cope, or does it look like no one works there as there is nothing left lying around? Is your visitor's chair alongside you or the other side of your desk? Every item and how it is placed can give out clues as to how you view yourself, or how you want others to view you. Take the time to occasionally check your work area layout and think about the impression it gives to others.

People will personalise their work area, to make it their own, by displaying various types of objects, such as family photographs, post-it notes, postcards, small models, mugs with a logo, executive toys, certificates of achievement, calendars, inspirational verses and cartoons. The list is endless but you need to consider what people's objects say about them, and what you display says about you.

Most of these items become 'wallpaper' after a while and are no longer noticed, so give thought to how you adorn your space and the messages it sends out. Too much clutter can make you look unorganised; cartoons and verses that are anti-authority, although humorous, can make you look like a rebel; the same old postcards and post-its could give the impression that you like things to stay as they are; and family pictures could make you look as if you have traditional values or are family focused.

Touch

Touch is an area that needs to be given consideration, as what you consider appropriate may not be interpreted in the same way by other people. We often communicate through touch, for example:

- the pat on the back to say 'well done';
- the welcoming handshake when we meet people;
- the guiding touch on someone's arm to steer them in the right direction.

If in doubt, the best approach is to avoid touching so that it cannot be misinterpreted. This is especially true when dealing with people from different cultures where your normal behaviour could cause offence.

Involuntary responses

We cannot prevent these responses from happening, or produce them voluntarily, although some can be mimicked. As we do not have any control over them, they provide us with a clear insight into the emotions of others. This is a two-edged sword, as it also means that our involuntary responses will reveal our true emotions to others.

Some examples are as follows:

- *Colour*: blushing, going pale;
- *Movement*: swallowing, nostrils flaring, trembling;
- *Skin*: sweaty, clammy;
- *Eyes*: blinking, tears;
- *Breathing*: heavy, rapid.

If we observe these responses in others or become aware of them in ourselves, we can consider the reason behind such an emotional reaction. When interacting with others, mentioning their involuntary responses can provide them with the opportunity to open up and express how they are feeling. There is a danger that it could also make them clam up and try to hide these responses, so judgment needs to be used.

Gestures

The use of gestures varies between cultures and countries, so care should be taken with the way we interpret them and the way we use them ourselves, especially if abroad or when hosting visitors from abroad or other cultures. What may be considered to be acceptable in one country could be offensive in another.

There are many familiar gestures that we use to communicate our feelings:

- *Downward glance*: modesty;
- *Wide eyes*: honesty or fear;
- *Rolling eyes upwards*: exasperation with a person or situation;
- *Raised eyebrows*: surprise.

Others include: clenched fist, nail biting, pointing or shaking a finger, pursed lips, rubbing chin, narrowing eyes, scratching head, hands on hips, sticking out tongue, tugging earlobe and waving.

We can determine people's attitudes by observing the amount and type of hand gestures used:

- Positive hand gestures are smooth and relaxed with the showing of the open-palms.
- Very sudden gestures can be seen as threatening, particularly if with clenched fists or showing the back of the hand.
- A lack of hand gestures can be seen as negative, as it shows an unwillingness to communicate fully or even that something is being withheld.

Gestures can be used instead of verbal communication. Finger, thumb or whole-hand gestures have a wide range of meanings, such as the thumb up or down, the OK sign and pointing. The meaning can vary between cultures and a positive gesture in one country can be viewed as an insult in another.

Personal space

Everyone requires their own personal space. This is an area around them, which should not be intruded upon as it makes people feel uncomfortable. They will often guard this space and feel threatened if it is encroached upon. This can result in an angry response or the person moving until they have enough space again. The distance can vary depending upon various factors, such as:

- *City or urban dweller*: City dwellers require a smaller area than those who live in the countryside. You can tell how much space a person requires by observing how far away they stand from other people. If you move into their personal space they will generally back away until they have regained sufficient space to make them feel comfortable again.

- *Country of origin*: Different countries adopt different distances so that some will generally stand closer than others. This can differ among genders.

- *The relationship with the person*: Close family members and loved ones will be allowed to get much closer than anyone else. People who we know socially will stand a little further away than family. Strangers will be expected to stand even further away. Women generally sit closer to one another than men do. We stand further away from people we do not like.

- *The space available*: People spread themselves out in the space available so they will end up closer together in a crowded pub and further apart in a park. This can lead to interesting situations when the space is too small, such as in a lift, where people compensate for the lack of space by not making eye contact etc.

Be aware of people's need for space and avoid encroaching on others while at work. Make sure you do not make them uncomfortable by standing over them, reading over their shoulders or moving your chair too close to theirs. Allow sufficient room for people to feel comfortable; if they move away slightly, do not start following them as they probably have a greater need for space than you do.

Space and power

Generally the more space we take up, the more powerful we feel and the more powerful we can appear to be to others. When people do not feel powerful they will usually try to take up less space, for example, people being told off will normally hang their head and keep their arms against their body, reducing their height and width. We also make ourselves appear smaller as a mark of respect when we are in the presence of someone we consider to be powerful, for example, when we bow in front of royalty.

Standing takes more space than sitting and can therefore make us appear more powerful. This is one reason why speakers stand while listeners remain seated. Indeed, it can be very difficult to take a speaker seriously if they are sitting.

Consider the different situations when height can be used to intimidate others, such as the policeman coming over to you in your car. While you remain sat in your car, he towers above you, and his height advantage adds to his control of the situation.

When you need to stand up in front of others, you can use this as an opportunity to appear powerful. Check your body language and make sure you are not undermining this advantage by stooping and looking uncomfortable. Stand upright and look confident to make the most of this advantage. Standing up can make you feel more assertive, so, where appropriate, consider standing when you are dealing with others. This even works when you are on the telephone, so next time you have a difficult call to make, try standing up to give yourself a boost.

Moving around means that you are taking up more space and this can come across as being in control, or even threatening, to other people in the room. By taking up more space than others, we increase our power and reduce theirs. Consider how lawyers will pace around the court room while putting across their point and trying to influence the jury.

We will not always be in a position to be able to stand and walk around. However, we can still give the impression of power when sitting by stretching out as far as possible with our arms and legs. Men may have the advantage here as it is not always possible for women to do this and still remain ladylike.

It is no coincidence that the higher up someone is in an organisation, the more space they are awarded. How much space you have is a status symbol – do not let others take it away, whether directly or indirectly. Your space will have an effect on how others perceive you, so make sure that you use all of the available space and try to expand your space further where possible. There is often spare space available so use your ingenuity to mark this as yours by moving work items into it, such as a waste basket, potted plant or coat stand. You can also move around within spare space on a regular basis to give the impression that all the space is yours.

We quite naturally require to work from a base that we can call our own. Even staff who share a desk will display personalised items while they are in situ. People will often hang a jacket over the chair to lay claim to that space while they are there. This can happen in more common areas, such as conference rooms and restaurants that we are only temporarily using.

Giving people the space they need

There will be times when it is more important to make sure that you provide the space that staff and customers need. This is when people feel emotionally or physically threatened and any invasion of their personal space will make the situation worse. This usually happens when they are facing a difficult situation, such as negotiating a contract, making a complaint, having an interview or taking part in an appraisal.

In these situations you need to make sure you keep your distance and provide plenty of space for them so that they do not feel overwhelmed or intimidated. In addition to allowing enough space for them to feel comfortable, check your own body posture to ensure this does not add to the situation. When people feel threatened, communication becomes very difficult as anxiety may start to affect the way they speak and think, making them defensive and resistant to what you are trying to achieve.

Building rapport

What is rapport?

Rapport is about building a relationship with another person so that you can relate to them in a way that makes them feel comfortable. We tend to like people who we consider to be similar to ourselves.

When we meet someone for the first time, socially, we will look for areas of common interest or try to find similarities in our backgrounds. Once we have established that these areas exist, we will then develop the relationship further, feeling safe in the knowledge that this is someone who is like us. If no common areas can be found, the relationship may not progress any further, as we may feel this is someone who we will not be able to get along with, as they are too different from ourselves and make us feel uncomfortable.

In work situations, we do not have the luxury of deciding who we wish to develop business relationships with based on who we feel comfortable with. We are expected to get along with people who we may avoid in a social situation. To be successful in these situations, we need to know how to build a rapport with someone so that they will feel comfortable with us and want to do business with us. By developing this skill you will be able to create a rapport with people in a few minutes, whether or not you like them, and even if you do not have areas of common interest.

Building rapport is a skill that can be developed based on the idea that people will like us if they think we are like them. This is done by matching our non-verbal communication to theirs. In this way, they will feel comfortable with us without knowing why. This occurs quite naturally when people already have a rapport with each other, as can be observed in social situations. When people like each other they will move in the same way. Observe how often couples attracted to each other will sip their drinks at the same time and adopt the same posture. Even their facial expressions will become similar.

Creating rapport

The aim is to match the other person's non-verbal behaviours. This should be done subtly; if the other person becomes aware of this matching behaviour they may feel they are being mimicked and respond negatively, possibly destroying any chance of a working relationship.

The following are areas where matching can take place. Rather than trying to match everything, start with one area and build up from there:

- *Breathing*: An easy way to match someone is to breathe at the same rate – breathe in and out when they do, matching the way they take their breaths.

- *Posture*: Be aware of how they position their body and take up a similar stance. If you copy them exactly it will look too obvious, so use a similar kind of body language, for example, open or closed.

- *Expression*: Facial expressions are easy to observe as this will be the area in which you are mainly focused, so match their mood and expression, are they concerned or enthusiastic?

- *Movement*: Observe how they move to see if it is, for example, slow and smooth or very lively and animated, and move in a similar manner. You can do this by following them when it is your turn to speak by using similar body movements to support your verbal communication. Slightly delaying your matching behaviour can help to make it less obvious.

- *Voice*: Take notice of their rate of speech, volume and tone of voice. If the other person is quietly spoken, drop the level of your voice. If they are very formal and polite in their speech then respond in a similar way.

It does not take very long to observe someone and then subtly mirror them, and yet this can make a major improvement in how we interact with colleagues and customers.

You may feel this is false or manipulative, however, this is about showing consideration for the way people prefer to communicate. It is often inappropriate to mismatch with people; for example, you will quite naturally show concern for someone who is upset, rather than carry on in an exuberant manner, as this would make you look callous. Similarly, if we insist on talking at a rapid pace when the other person likes to take their time, we could make them feel uncomfortable. Rapport is about respecting their feelings and responding in a way that demonstrates an understanding of their position.

Once you have established rapport with someone, you can try encouraging them to change their behaviour, when this is desirable. This can be used, for example, to help people start to relax if they appear apprehensive. This is achieved by starting to take the lead and see if they will follow. If you are dealing with someone who is using closed body language you can slowly move towards a more open posture and see if they follow. Always start by mirroring their position before gradually moving to the desired state. People will often follow on a subconscious level, once we have built a rapport with them. Helping them to adopt a more open pose will in turn help them to relax and have a more open attitude. If they do not follow, you need to go back to mirroring and then try again. This can be used in many situations when we need to change a person's behaviour when it is preventing us from helping them, such as helping to calm someone who is making a complaint.

You will find that you naturally have rapport with someone whose company you enjoy. Become more aware of how this is achieved in your own social life so that you can develop this skill in the workplace. This is a skill that can be learned with practice and one that you could try out with friends and family, to gain confidence. As with all personal development, you should aim to make improvements gradually until you become competent rather than expecting to succeed overnight.

Meeting and greeting people

In business we need to be able to interact with what is often an extremely wide section of people. Being able to meet and greet is one of the skills that you need to be able to master. The rise in electronic communication can mean that we only occasionally meet people face to face, so it becomes even more important to get it right when we do.

By creating a good first impression, you can start business relationships on the right footing and make it easier to continue on this basis. A bad start will mean that you will be continually trying to regain your position and will be unable to relax and enjoy the meeting.

Prepare yourself

- Before you meet your guest or host, check your clothes and prepare your posture so that you are in an upright balanced position.

- Check your breathing; if you are nervous take a few long deep breaths in though the nose and out though the mouth – this should help you to feel calmer.

- Put a confident look on your face that is charming and intelligent. Be prepared to look pleased to see the person you are meeting and greeting.

- Transfer anything you are carrying, such as a bag or folder, to your left hand so that you are free to shake hands.

- Study any doors to make sure you know how they will open.

Make your entrance

- Enter the room or reception area as if you have a right to be there – walk briskly but not in a rushed manner.

- Try to close the door behind you without turning around, if possible.

- Look pleased to be there – approach your visitor or host with a smile and make eye contact.

- Say their name and give yours while offering your right hand for a handshake – give sufficient warning of the handshake by extending your hand from a few paces away.

- Keep your arms to your sides and supply open gestures to steer your visitor towards the lift or office – keep all your movements smooth and well coordinated.

Presentation skills

Your body language plays an important part in any presentation. Your audience will be aware of your body language, usually at a subconscious level, and will certainly be aware of it at a conscious level if you make any glaring mistakes, such as fidgeting, speaking too quietly or appearing frozen. You may have prepared a wonderful presentation, but if this is badly presented in terms of your body language, then the audience may not be able to understand you, be distracted or find you unconvincing.

From the moment you start your presentation, you need to focus on your body language and not let this slip until the presentation – including any question and answer session – is over. Take the time to practise your presentation, not only in terms of what you say, but also how you are going to say it, including how you will use visual aids, such as flipcharts or acetates.

Here are some main points to consider:

- *Personal space*: As already discussed, people need to be surrounded by a certain amount of personal space, and if this space is invaded then they will begin to feel uncomfortable. This also applies to audiences, and therefore you should not stand to close to them. You should allow at least ten feet distance between you; however, a large audience may require more space. The distance between you and your audience is also important so that everyone can see you clearly and you have sufficient area to deliver your presentation.

- *Posture*: The way you stand will be one of the first things your audience will notice, and from this they will immediately begin to make assumptions. Your posture needs to convey confidence and authority so they feel it is going to be worth listening to you. When you stand up, you will raise yourself above the level of the audience, immediately giving you importance and the opportunity to be taken seriously. The way you stand will also have an influence on the audience. Stand tall in an evenly balanced position. Try not to slope forward as this can appear dominating. This can often happen when you are trying to stress a point. Do not lean to one side, as this can make you look awkward, unsure or not convinced by your own message. Aim for an upright, balanced and open stance which suggests confidence and a belief in your message.

- *Movement*: Standing still can bore an audience, as their gaze will need to stay focused in one direction. By using appropriate body language with relaxed natural movements that add emphasis and interest to your talk, your audience will move their eyes to follow you, thus avoiding the boredom of looking at the same place all the time. Do not go to the other extreme of displaying too much movement by dancing around and waving your arms, as this will be too distracting and annoying. All your movements should be calm and smooth. Practise how you will move around while delivering your speech beforehand until it appears natural and confident. Ask others to observe you and provide feedback, if possible, as you may have some annoying habits you are unaware of.

- *Dress*: How you dress will depend upon the expectations of your audience, so you need to do some research before choosing your outfit. To be taken seriously, you need to look the part, and come across as confident and knowledgeable, so consider dressing slightly above the level of the audience to establish a professional image. This may not always be the case, for example, if you are addressing people in higher authority than yourself, such as the Board of Directors, you may not wish to out do them; while you need to project the right image to establish your credibility, you do not want them to wonder how much they are paying you.

  As a representative of your profession, you may be asked to give a talk, perhaps at a career convention, school, or women's institute. In which case, you need to look the part by wearing the normal working attire, such as a uniform or business suit.

  When you have chosen your outfit, ensure it is clean and in a good state of repair. Wear your outfit when practising your speech – make sure you can move around comfortably and that your clothes move with you, for example, when pointing to the top of a flipchart. If you buy something new for an important presentation, make sure you 'wear it in' beforehand, especially shoes, as you could otherwise end up in discomfort or even pain.

- *Eye contact*: Making the correct amount eye contact with an audience is essential when giving a presentation. If it is not correctly used it can give out negative messages, as a lack of it will make you appear distant from and uninterested in your audience. By not maintaining eye contact you will 'switch off' the audience and they will then lose interest in what you are saying. A lack of eye contact could also make you appear to be untrustworthy or unsure of yourself.

  Eye contact is one of the main forms of non-verbal communication, and needs to be used positively, to gain and maintain people's attention. You can do this by looking around the audience and maintaining eye contact with people for a few seconds at a time. Be sure to look around the whole audience rather than just those at the front or in the middle. Do not avoid making eye contact with members of the audience who appear to be uninterested or hostile, include them as well so that they feel involved. Your eye contact needs to be gentle and relaxed; avoid staring at people as this will come across as hostile.

- *Match the needs of the audience*: You will need to establish a rapport with your audience, which again comes down to research. Establish the reason for your presentation so that it will be appropriate to the needs of the audience. This can involve many different aspects:

  - *Purpose*: Is the purpose of the presentation to inform or persuade? Most presentations fall into one of these two categories, so make sure that your presentation is appropriate to the purpose. For example, if the aim is persuade the Board to give approval for a project then you need to make sure you sell the benefits of the idea to them with some very persuasive arguments, rather than just giving them all the details.

- *Content*: Are there any particular areas to be covered? Some subjects can be wide ranging so find out if any aspects need to be covered so that you do not miss these out of your preparation. People are usually asked to give a presentation to meet a particular need so make sure you know what it is.

- *Timing*: How long should the presentation last? If it is part of a conference involving many other speakers, then timing is vital and you need to ensure you do not finish short or overrun. Time your practice sessions until you get it right.

- *Level*: What is the knowledge level of the audience? Will this be an awareness session for people with no previous knowledge, or are you presenting to a group of experts? This will determine the level at which you pitch your speech, in terms of how much you need to explain and how much detail you can go into. It also determines how much jargon and the kind of technical terms that can be used.

- *Type of audience*: Are the audience there voluntarily or not? In some work situations, staff are often expected to attend training sessions that may not interest them. If this is the case, you will need to work hard to sell the benefit of the session and make the subject as interesting as possible. Bear in mind that you cannot force people to be interested, so do not take it personally when people appear uninterested or lack your enthusiasm.

- *Voice*: Speak at a steady pace so that you come across as confident and relaxed. Direct your talk towards the audience. If you are using notes, then practise so that you only need to glance down occasionally. Make sure that all the audience can hear you clearly, either by speaking loud enough or adjusting any amplifying equipment. Vary your pitch by raising and lowering it as you go along, rather than speaking in a monotone which will send people to sleep. Avoid going up at the end of every sentence, as this will make it appear like a question or that you are unsure of what you are saying. Appear authoritative by making your statements go down at the end.

- *Dealing with nerves*: Even people who regularly deliver presentations can still suffer from nerves, thereby having an undesired effect on their performance. You can reduce your feelings of anxiety by making sure you have a well prepared and rehearsed presentation. Good planning reduces the likelihood of things going wrong. For example, make yourself familiar with the room layout and how any equipment works.

  Be aware of your body language and aim to look confident and overcome any signs of nervousness that may suddenly decide to express themselves, such as fidgeting, waffling or jangling things in your pocket. Take your time and take deep breaths to calm yourself down. It may be an idea to have a glass of water available so that you can take a sip if your mouth goes dry. This can also give you a chance to collect your thoughts.

- *Using visual aids*: Always practise beforehand so that you can provide a slick performance with any visual aids you choose to use. Here are some tips on most of the common ones used:

  - *Cue cards*: These are the small cards on which you have written the key points from your speech so that you can elaborate on them during your presentation. Number these in one of the corners so that if they are dropped, they can easily put be put back in order. If possible, tie them together loosely through a hole in one corner so that they stay together but enable you leaf through them one at a time.

- *Acetates*: Make sure you are not stood in the way of the projected screen, thereby spoiling the view of the audience. Do not put too much information on these, only show key points on which you can elaborate. Put numbers on the acetates so that you can easily put them in order. Point to the acetate with a pointer or pen if you wish to guide your audience through the points, rather than pointing to the projected screen as you will obscure the audiences' view. Switch off the equipment when not in use, as it will become a distraction.

- *Flipchart*: Try to face the front as much as possible by standing to the side and leaning over to write on the flipchart rather than showing your back to the audience. If you know in advance what you are going to write or draw, pencil it in lightly, so that you can follow this on the day with the marker pen and ensure it is neat, level and well spaced. If you are using it to record ideas from the audience then lightly draw some lines in pencil to help ensure your writing stays level, as it is very easy to start sloping upwards or downwards.

- ▪ *Handling questions*: This is where good preparation pays off as you must know your subject area well if you are providing a presentation. Make it clear at the beginning of your presentation when you will take questions. Are you happy to take them throughout the session, or is your audience expected to wait till the end? When asked a question, repeat it so that the whole audience can hear it, and address your answer to whole audience. This ensures that the audience is kept interested and it is less likely for one person to monopolise you by keep asking questions as you will not be maintaining eye contact with them. You cannot be expected to know everything. If you do not know the answer, praise the question and offer to find out. If it is outside the scope of your talk then say so. If someone disagrees with you and tries to be argumentative do not get drawn into an argument but suggest that there are different viewpoints and that you may have to agree to differ. If no one asks any questions you can overcome the embarrassing silence by offering to be available during a break, lunch or for a short time afterwards so that people can approach you on an individual basis. You can also make this offer if there are too many questions and you are running out of time.

Team meetings and briefings

One of the main challenges as a manager is to ensure that staff are well briefed so they can understand the organisation's objectives, feel part of any changes and are clear on the part they are to play.

Any time spent with your team is quality time and should be treated as such. By updating your team and giving them the chance to raise any issues you are giving out non-verbal messages that say your staff are important to you. You can show how you value them by making sure they are kept fully informed and are given the opportunity to provide valuable feedback.

Managers often feel they are too busy to provide team meetings and fail to put in the necessary preparation to make them relevant and interesting. This leads to the staff appearing bored and uninterested which confirms the manager's belief that team meetings are not worth the effort, which in turns leads to team meetings being either cancelled or still being badly prepared. Staff then complain about not knowing what is going on and this leads to poor morale within the area.

- *Select the information to be used*: As a leader, you need to ensure team meetings are carried out regularly and provide information which is relevant and pitched at the right level. You should not swamp staff with all the information you receive. Select information you are going to use and explain how it is relevant to your staff. Make sure that minutes are provided for those who did not attend and brief them separately on any important issues.

- *Sell the message*: Put information across in a positive manner even if it is not good news. People are often afraid of any changes that are to be made. Team meetings give you the opportunity to sell the positive aspects and address any concerns they may have.

- *Check staff participation*: During your team meetings, your staff will be communicating with you, even when they do not speak. They will all express through their body language how they are feeling or thinking. They will show whether they are interested in the item under discussion and whether they agree with what is being said. Staff who are interested will display this by looking attentive, leaning forward, nodding and may even mirror the posture of the team leader. Lack of interest will be shown by sitting back, doodling, looking around or staring through the windows. By observing these responses you will gain an idea about the likely division of opinion.

- *Positions within the team*: You can become more aware of what is happening at team meetings by observing your staff. Take notice of where staff sit and how they position themselves with each other. Usually people will sit in the same place, which can denote the pecking order within the team.

- *Negative team behaviour*: Look out for any negative body language which may suggest that staff are not happy within the team. This will include sitting far away from the others, with their bodies not directly facing the team and only speaking when spoken to. Crossing their arms and legs, which is a closed body position, can either show a negative attitude or disagreement with what is being said. If they whisper or signal to another member of the team this can be distracting and make the others feel left out.

  As the team leader, you need to discourage these negative behaviours by gaining the commitment of staff and encouraging them to become more involved. This may need to be done outside the team meeting and take a period of time. Use your facilitation skills to ensure that no one dominates the meeting and no one is left out. Aim to gain a balanced contribution from your team.

- *See and be seen*: Make sure that all staff can clearly see you. A round table is ideal, but if this is not possible, try to be as central as possible. This will also mean that you can see all your staff, which will be important for picking up on their non-verbal behaviours. Face the group to show that you are available to them and that you are giving them your full attention.

- *Use open body language*: Speak clearly in a confident manner and use body language to support the messages you are putting across. For example, if you cross your arms and/or legs you will appear to be uninterested, so make sure your body language is open to demonstrate that you are willing to listen.

- *Watch their body language*: Become familiar with the body language of the team so that you understand the responses being made. Notice their facial expressions, posture and gestures as these will provide you with more feedback about how things are going than anything they actually say.

- *Be seen to be fair*: Respond to what others say in an even-handed way and avoid being seen to have any 'favourites'. Use your body language to show that you are alert and listening to what is being said when others speak. Encourage your team to speak more by using non-verbal signals, such as nodding and smiling.

- *Use eye contact*: Make eye contact evenly with all team members throughout the meeting and watch for any responses to what is being said by yourself and others. If you avoid looking at anyone they will feel left out and wonder if they should be there in the future.

- *Involve everyone*: Not all staff will venture an opinion in a team meeting. Staff who remain silent may have a valid point. If they are not invited to speak, they may instead discuss this outside the meeting. If this happens, you will not be aware of everyone's opinions and can end up making a bad decision as a result. By observing your team you will be able to invite team members to express their views when their non-verbal signals indicate they have a point of view, such as smiling and nodding if positive or shoulder shrugging or sighing deeply if negative.

- *Dealing with emotions*: When communication takes place it usually involves our emotions. Most of the time, these will be under control and not present a problem. Occasionally when changes are suggested or complaints discussed, these can lead to staff feeling quite strongly and displaying their emotions by looking angry, sulking, and speaking loudly etc. These situations can have an influence on the rest of the team and make them uncomfortable and less willing to communicate. Indeed, you may need to stop the open discussion and offer to discuss the issue on an individual basis or suggest leaving it to the next meeting and offer to find out more information in the meantime.

Attending meetings

A large proportion of a manager's time is spent in meetings, whether in a group situation or on a one-to-one basis. This is time that needs to be spent effectively, yet managers often feel as if this time is being stolen from them, and that they have no control over this. Meetings they attend go on for too long and are seemingly unproductive. Having so much time tied up in meetings leaves them little time for other aspects of their role, and as a result their performance suffers or they end up working long hours to compensate. All meetings should be regularly reviewed to ensure they are necessary and run as efficiently as possible. Before going to a meeting, you need to assess why you are attending and what you hope to gain from it. You can begin by considering the following:

- *Do you need to attend?* Your success in attending meetings starts well before the meeting takes place. Meetings can take up a large part of a manager's time so the first thing you need to consider is, do you really need to attend? And, if so, do you need to attend all of it? If you turn up for every meeting you are invited to, it can make you look too available, and will leave you less time to fulfil all your other duties.

- *Preparing for meetings*: Once you have decided it is necessary for you to attend, go through the agenda and decide what you want to get out of the meeting. Make notes on what contribution you are going to make on any agenda items. Canvas the opinions of other attendees to check their position to gauge the support for any items you are interested in. You may need to do some work on persuading others to understand the issues involved before the meeting.

- *Arriving at meetings*: This is where you can put into effect the work you have done on your image. Do not assume that just because you are meeting with your colleagues that you do not have to make an effort. Create and maintain a good image by making sure you get the basics right:

  - arrive in good time, but not too early as this gives the impression you have too much spare time;

  - if you are late keep calm and briefly apologise without going into too much detail;

  - make a good entrance by looking confident and positive;

  - greet the other attendees in a friendly manner but keep it brief;

  - choose where you sit taking into account the effect this can have. This is covered in more detail later.

- *During the meeting*: Always give the meeting your full attention by not indulging in any behaviour that may be distracting, such as shuffling papers, whispering to others, pouring drinks. Make sure any mobile phones, pagers and bleepers are switched off. It is unfair on the speaker to be interrupted by unnecessary noises and makes you look unorganised, uninterested and discourteous.

Actively listen to everything that is being said so that if someone asks you something you will not be caught out. This will also ensure that when you do speak your comments are relevant.

Respond to what is being said by smiling when you agree, looking concerned when you disagree and puzzled if the message is unclear. In this way whoever is speaking will know how things are going and can respond as necessary, for example, by explaining further if everyone is looking puzzled.

Do not take too many notes as this will stop you from being involved in the meeting and interacting with others, it will also make you appear subservient. The same applies to pouring drinks for others or passing round refreshments which will lower your status in front of others.

- *Getting to speak*: If you are nervous about speaking, try to say something early on so that you become more confident about speaking in front of others and more willing to say something later when you want to make an important point.

  You may need to use your body language to show that you want to speak. This can be done in several ways so observe how others do this to find out what is acceptable. You could try leaning forward and making eye contact with the chairperson or slightly raising your hand or a pen.

  Women will usually take it in turns to speak and often invite quiet members to speak. This does not happen with men who 'overtalk' each other. In business meetings you may need to start talking as the current speaker is about to finish. If you wait for a gap, this may never come and you will give some else the opportunity to cut in. If you find it difficult to find the opportunity to speak, it is worth developing your reputation, as people are more likely to want to hear from those whose opinion they value. When you do speak, make sure that you keep to the point and speak in a positive and concise manner. In this way, others will be more willing to give you the chance to speak. Most people will try to avoid giving the floor to those who are negative or long-winded.

- *When you speak*: Use positive body language to support your message. Use eye contact by looking at everyone in turn to maintain their attention. Keep a pleasant expression and use open gestures to demonstrate your conviction and confidence in what is being said. Vary your voice so that you sound interesting. Avoid any negative body language that may undermine your message, such as fidgeting, apologising or head shaking.

- *At the end of the meeting*: Pack up swiftly and leave in the same positive way that you arrived. Avoid ambushing people to talk to them about something you wish to discuss, as they may need to be somewhere else fairly soon. Instead, make an arrangement to contact or meet with them. Do not collect up any spare refreshments to take back with you as this makes you look greedy and cheap.

- *Power seats*: Where you sit at a meeting can make a big difference to how you are perceived and your chances of being listened to. For example, the chairperson will sit either at one end of the table or in the middle of one of the long sides. They will usually choose the seat which faces the door so they can see people as they arrive. You will need to find out where they sit before taking your place as if you sit directly opposite the chairperson this can be seen as confrontational. Sitting directly opposite widthways makes you very visible to the extent that the chairperson will try to ignore you as if they are always looking straight across at you the others will feel left out.

The seat to the side of the chairperson is usually reserved for their supporting staff, such as their deputies. This position is one of silent support, the 'right hand man'. When someone in this seat speaks they will be seen as a spokesperson. This position is also in the chairperson's blind spot so you should avoid sitting here unless you have a supporting role.

The best position to aim for is to the side of the middle position nearest the chairperson so that you do not look like you are trying to be on their side or challenging them. If you sit further beyond the middle point then you are too distant and will find it difficult to gain attention and be heard.

Gaining cooperation

When you achieve a supervisory position, you will not automatically gain everyone's cooperation through your new-found authority. You will still need the goodwill of your team and to persuade colleagues and higher management, if you are to be effective. These are some of the ways in which by using your non-verbal skills you can gain their cooperation:

- *Put yourself in their shoes*: Try to see things from their point of view and demonstrate your concern for their feelings. Explain how their role fits into the bigger picture and how their contribution plays a part in the success of the whole team and can contribute to achieving their aims, such as improving their working life or career progression.

- *Make them feel understood*: Take the time to listen to their concerns so that you can overcome any objections and provide reassurance if necessary. They may have valid points to make so be prepared to be flexible. Show that you value their opinions and are willing to do your best for them; this will create a good working relationship in which they are more likely to cooperate.

- *Involve them in decisions where possible*: When people have the chance to be involved, they will understand how the decision has been reached and be more likely to cooperate. As adults, we cannot all expect to get our own way the whole time, but if we believe the decision has been arrived at fairly then it is more likely to be accepted.

- *Aim to win the war not just one battle*: If you win an argument or get your own way through using your authority, you may feel like you have won, but this is only a short-term gain. In future, people will be less willing to cooperate with you and can even make things difficult for you. It is better to lead by consensus than power. There is usually 'more than one way to skin a cat', so look for all available options and choose one that most closely matches the majority view rather than your own preferred solution.

- *Create the vision*: Help people to change by showing them the way forward and convincing them that it is possible to achieve it. Most people resist change as they are more comfortable with the current way of working. You need to sell the benefits and reassure them by clearly showing how they will be supported during the period of change. This will help overcome any feelings of uncertainty over the future.

- *Timing*: Time any requests well, so they have more chance of success. Be aware of what is happening so that you do not approach people when they are not feeling their best or have just had some bad news. Choose moments when they are more likely to be receptive and this will increase the likelihood of a positive outcome.

Staff appraisal

Staff appraisals should be a positive experience, as the meeting is about building upon what has happened over the last year and consolidating the feedback that has already been regularly given. There should be nothing unexpected as any negative issues will have been addressed at the appropriate time. Unfortunately this is not always the case, and appraisals can sometimes end up being difficult for both parties.

Staff appraisal should form part of an overall performance management system with:

- clearly agreed team and individual objectives in place;

- systems of monitoring in place that are visible and understood by all;

- regular feedback sessions so that staff can be motivated through praise being given for good performance and support being provided where there is a development need.

Giving positive feedback is relatively easy, but giving negative feedback can cause some managers to feel uncomfortable and defensive. This can be overcome by ensuring that any feedback is based on facts and observations rather than personal opinions. The way we provide feedback will tell our staff how we value them and where our priorities are, so it is important we do this in a way that creates the right impression. The following are some areas to consider:

- *Preparation*: Prepare some key points in advance, so that you are clear on the areas to be covered. Practise what you are going to say, as it is often hard to put written notes into normal conversation, especially when you are feeling under pressure.

- *Start with the positive*: Go through the good points first so that members of staff feel valued and more at ease. Once in this frame of mind they will be more willing to accept a few criticisms and more likely to agree to action to improve these areas. This needs to be done subtly, as if it becomes obvious that you are only giving praise so that you can criticise them, they will be wary of any future praise you may give. Any praise should be valid and appropriate to the situation.

- *Be specific*: Give precise details so there is enough information to show why the point is being made and where improvement needs to be made. Staff cannot learn from general comments and these will often lead to disagreements in which you may have no real evidence to support your case. This will lead to you losing face and the member of staff feeling badly treated.

- *Be selective*: There are always areas for improvement so prioritise the main ones, rather than trying to tackle a long list of trivial items. A development plan with a few focused areas for action is more likely to succeed than one that overwhelms people.

- *Take ownership*: You should take ownership of the feedback offered. We often rely on other staff to provide us with useful feedback on staff performance or it could come from customers. You decide on the feedback you give, so you need to be convinced of it. Use the word 'I' to show you are taking responsibility for it, do not give the impression you are just passing on what others have said and that you may not agree with it.

- *Involve them in the change*: There is always the temptation to suggest how they can make improvements according to our own preferences. Staff may resist the need to change, and feel it is being imposed on them, so involve them in how they can make changes and try to offer choices so that they feel in control of their development.

- *Body language*: Show that you are in control of the meeting by the use of positive body language. This needs to be maintained even when providing negative feedback so that you do not undermine the messages you give out. Use assertive eye contact with an open body posture. Keep calm and maintain smooth movements, using slow nods when listening. Lean slightly forward when giving negative feedback to show that you are serious but do not overdo this so that you look aggressive.

- *Give sufficient notice*: Staff should be given about two weeks' notice so they have the chance to think about the meeting and prepare themselves.

- *Environmental barriers*: If you sit opposite each other with a desk or table in between, this will form a subconscious barrier and may appear confrontational. If you must have a desk or table, try and sit side by side or either side of a corner.

- *Interruptions*: do not allow any interruptions to take place as this shows you do not consider the meeting to be serious and that your member of staff is not important to you. This is their quality time with you and should be treated as such. Plan to make sure you are left in peace by:
  - stopping or diverting all telephone calls;
  - putting a notice on the door;
  - asking someone else to stand in for your role.
- *Allow enough time*: You need to both be relaxed and not worry about running out of time. Allow plenty of time to carry out the appraisal and complete the paperwork afterwards.

Negotiating skills

Successful negotiation requires you to be aware of the three phases of non-verbal communication. These phases are:

- What is their body language telling you?
- What is your body language telling them?
- How are you going to respond to manage both?

Observing them

When you are negotiating with someone either internally or externally, observing their non-verbal signals can provide you with useful information. Keep a close eye on them throughout the meeting, as it is through noting the changes in their body language, that you will be able to determine how things are really going.

If you are dealing with people you are not familiar with, you will need to determine their normal body language so that you can notice any changes that take place. The best time to observe this is during the opening stages of the meeting when pleasantries are exchanged and rapport building takes place.

There are some non-verbal clues which can signal there may be a problem or that they have a hidden agenda; these include nervous gestures, such as:

- biting the lip;

- excessive blinking;

- rapid breathing which can be seen by their shoulder movements;

- hands near or touching the mouth;

- stroking the nose;

- jumpy movements;

- moving away if they do not like you or disagree with you;

- moving from side to side and shifting weight about, which can show uncertainty or nervousness.

There may be some positive signs which give an indication that they are being friendly and open to your ideas. These would include:

- welcoming gestures that flow naturally;

- smiling to show they are feeling confident and in agreement with you;

- opening palms towards you simultaneously;

- leaning forward to show progress is being made;

- moving closer to you, showing they like you or agree with you.

You will need to notice the non-verbal signals that are being sent to you. Is their body in a closed or open position? Are they making regular eye contact? Do they constantly fidget and move around? If they do appear to be defensive or nervous, you will become aware of this even though you may not know the reason. You need to decide how to handle these signals. Are you going to ask if there are any issues they wish to raise or are you going to wait and see if they tell you anyway? Are you going to change your body language to try and influence them to change theirs?

As the meeting progresses, you will be able to tell if there are any changes in their non-verbal signals. By noticing these behavioural changes, you will be able to interpret the possible meanings. These changes may signal that they do not agree with you or are not interested in what you are proposing. They may start to use body language that breaks off their contact with you, such as losing eye contact, turning their body away and sighing heavily. When this happens you need to try and re-engage their attention by either asking if they wish to make any comments or by providing a break to give them a chance to refresh themselves and give you the opportunity to think things through and decide on a new strategy.

To observe them closely, you need to ensure you maintain eye contact without staring at them. Use friendly glances and open body posture. People are often distracted by paperwork and spend too much time checking their notes instead of focusing on the other party. If they pass you something to read, ask for a verbal summary so that you can maintain your observations. By keeping your attention on them you will be able to tell by their behaviour if what they are telling you is in keeping with their non-verbal signals.

Being self-aware

While observing others and becoming aware of all the non-verbal messages they are sending out, you will start to realise that you are doing the same. In addition to observing and interpreting people's non-verbal clues you need to check your own.

Aim to build rapport and maintain positive body language so that the outcome of the negotiation is more likely to be successful. You need to come across as honest and receptive. This can be accomplished by using, at the very least, the following open signals:

- keep your body facing them;
- maintain regular eye contact;
- keep your arms and legs uncrossed;
- keep your feet flat and pointing forward;
- lean slightly forward.

By using open and positive non-verbal language you are showing your willingness to be receptive to the negotiations.

Managing your body language and theirs

Use mirroring to put the other side at ease by matching them in a subtle way. This will help to create a friendly and relaxed atmosphere.

Give the impression that you are receptive to their ideas, when they are speaking, by smiling and nodding as they go through their main points. When they finish speaking, remain silent while still appearing attentive and this may encourage them to provide more information. Be aware that body language works both ways and they can use the same tactics on you to gain more information.

Negotiations can be of major importance, and while under pressure to reach the desired solution, it can be tempting to try and analyse and interpret everything that is happening. Most people will be initially nervous, so give them the chance to settle down before drawing any negative conclusions, and make sure you look for groups of clues in their behaviour rather than attaching too much importance to one single gesture.

Attending interviews

When attending an interview, everything that you do and say is on show to be analysed consciously and subconsciously. You only have a short time to make a good personal impact. You will be expected not only to look good but to communicate well both verbally and visually. Interviewers will gain many of their impressions from your posture, dress and gestures about your ability and suitability for the position.

You need to concentrate on your non-verbal communication from arrival to departure. Do not assume that you only need to impress the interviewers as there may be other staff whose opinion may be sought, such as the receptionist or secretary who greets you and takes you to the interview room.

The correct use of posture, movement and facial expressions will help you to make a positive impression on everyone that you meet.

- *Forward planning*: Your pre-interview work is vital. You need to know how you will come across and how you want to be perceived. Planning should start weeks before the interview itself, when possible. Find out as much as you can about the company you are approaching and its culture. If possible, go and take a look a few days beforehand.

- *Choosing an outfit*: Your outfit will play a major part in the impact that you make, so it worth taking the time and effort to make sure you get it right. When considering your outfit it is important to also focus on the smaller details that can easily let you down if you are not careful. Your outfit needs to be smart, well-made and preferably understated, as you want them to notice you rather than your clothes. You should always wear a good pair of business-like shoes that are in a good state of repair and have been cleaned. If you carry a bag, make sure it is easy to use and only has the essentials in it including a pen and notepaper. Check the overall impression that your whole outfit makes to ensure it is well coordinated and practise being able to move around in it comfortably.

- *Getting there*: Unless you are very familiar with the venue, you will need to check how to get there and preferably have a practice run in similar traffic conditions. Allow plenty of time for your journey so that any slight delays can be taken in your stride. It is better to arrive early than end up rushing in the last minute, leaving yourself flustered. If you do arrive too early, this time can be used to read through your notes before going into the building so that you can arrive 10–15 minutes early.

- *Building rapport*: It is now fairly well known that mirroring the interviewer will help to make them feel more positive to the person being interviewed. It is worth reading the previous section on building rapport in addition to the main points included here.

  The idea of mirroring is based on the fact that we tend to like people who are similar to ourselves. When we are talking to people that we like, we naturally mirror them, as can be seen at many social functions. By subtly imitating the interviewers' body language you can create a more friendly and relaxed environment. Subtly is key, as any clumsy efforts will be immediately noticed and can even appear offensive if it looks like you are mimicking them. Aim to observe their posture, movements and speech and gradually reflect this back to them so they feel comfortable with you.

- *Reading their body language*: By observing the interviewer you will be able to pick up on their non-verbal signals that indicate how they are reacting to you. By interpreting these clues you will be able to identify their thoughts and feelings and adjust your responses accordingly. The section on body language will help you to learn about the different non-verbal signals and how these may be interpreted.

- *Posture*: Most interviews are carried out in a seated position so the way you sit is your opportunity to give a positive impression. Practise how you sit before the interview so that it will come across quite naturally and confidently.

One of the key areas to consider is how to place your arms and legs, especially as these may suddenly feel as if they do not belong to you when you are nervous. With your arms, start by resting on the arms of the chair and keep your hands lower than your elbows. To start with, try not to move your arms and hands too much as this will give the impression of being calm and confident. Our legs also need to give an appearance of confidence and this can be achieved by either crossing at the ankles or by having one foot slightly forward and the other under the chair giving an impression of being alert. The legs should never be crossed higher up as this creates a barrier and makes you appear negative and defensive.

- *Eye contact*: Eye contact with the interviewer is an essential part of any interview. Without it the interviewer will feel remote from you and is unlikely to relate to you in a meaningful way. Eye contact should be a positive form of non-verbal communication, but if it is not used correctly it can easily become negative. Keep your eye contact constant while listening and vary it slightly while talking. It is a good idea to look away thoughtfully during the pause after they have asked a question and you have formed the answer. This gives the impression that the question was a good one and that you are being honest in your answer.

- *Movement*: Try to limit your own movements slightly at the start of the interview. The interviewer will be looking at you and working on first impressions. The start and finish of an interview can be the most dangerous times. Sit well in the seat, engage in a little small talk but be prepared to listen, rather than gush.

- *Laughter*: Keep your laughter to a minimum. Nervous laughter will undermine the confident image you have worked so hard to portray. Smile and use a polite laugh when appropriate, and avoid laughing too loudly or readily.

- *Drinks*: In some interviews you will be asked if you want a drink. Often a glass of water is provided, especially if you are expected to make a short presentation. Taking the occasional sip of water can help with your nerves by relieving a dry mouth and giving you the opportunity to pause and think.

  Tea and coffee, however, are another matter, as if you spill or drip these on your clothes you will have ruined the positive image you have worked so hard to create. Hot drinks can also pose other problems, such as when you are going to drink. This is not easy to do while you are speaking and you will look distracted if drinking while listening to them.

- *Listening*: Do not forget to use your listening skills while at an interview. A good impression can be maintained while listening in the following ways:

  - match your facial expression to what they are saying, for example, show concern;

  - smile and nod when appropriate;

  - keep your hands closed to stop any fidgeting;

  - lean forward to show interest;

  - do not over-respond to what is being said or you could look false.

- *Pauses*: Pauses will happen in interviews and can be unnerving. They may make you feel that someone should be saying something to fill the void, and wondering if it should be you. You will need to relax and keep calm when pauses happen so that you do not end up gibbering away. Accept that pauses will happen and that you need to even create a few of your own. You may need to pause after being asked a question so that you can provide a considered response rather than the first thing that comes into your head. Interviewers often need time to write things down or check their file. Often interviewers will pause when you have finished answering a question and the temptation here is to assume they want more information which leads to you trying to carry on. In this instance it may be better to ask if there are any aspects of your answer that require more explanation.

- *Ending the interview*: At the end of most interviews you will be asked if you have any questions before they finish off with the usual confirmation of when a decision will be made etc. This is your opportunity to ask any interesting questions you have prepared or confirm that everything has been covered during the interview. Calmly smile and wait until the interviewer gets up, at which point you should rise in a unhurried manner. Pick up any belongings, while making sure your hand is free for any handshake that is offered. Thank them as you leave.

  Sometimes they may gesture that the interview is over and do not move to show you out. In this case, rise calmly and smile at them for a brief moment. If they do not offer to shake hands, turn and make your own way out.

Other cultures

People from different cultures and countries to your own may have different norms when it comes to non-verbal communication. This presents a problem, as what you may consider to be normally acceptable, may cause offence to others. This can be quite disastrous in a work situation, as we cannot assume that everyone will take the 'when in Rome...' attitude, and we need to show consideration for the customs and values of all our staff and customers. When we do not know what will be expected of us, we need to find out beforehand by contacting a library, the appropriate embassy or any other reliable source of such information. You could always ask the person concerned in the same way that you would ask about any other differences in requirements.

When there is a language barrier, our non-verbal communication becomes even more important, as at times, it may be the only way in which we can communicate. When we concentrate on understanding another language, we start to rely more on how things are said to help us. Often under these circumstances people start to use more exaggerated body language to help get across their message, such as gesticulating more, varying facial expressions constantly and adding extra expression to their voice.

Some areas you need to consider are:

- *Personal space*: The requirement for personal space will vary from culture to culture and will differ according to the relationship. It is best to let the other person be our guide, by allowing them stand at a distance comfortable to them, and then making sure we maintain that distance.

- *Gestures*: Some cultures will use a lot of gestures and movements when talking, so they come across as highly animated, while others do not and may come across as reserved. While it would be difficult to try and match either of these, if it is not our normal behaviour, it is possible to move towards these extremes by becoming either slightly more or less animated than usual.

    The meaning of gestures can vary, so you need to check in order to avoid unknowingly giving offence. Even the 'yes' and 'no' gestures are not the same throughout the world. If there is uncertainty, then it is best to avoid using gestures or at least keep them to a minimum to reduce the risk.

- *Eye contact*: Making direct eye contact is usually interpreted as a sign of being open and honest; however, in some other cultures it can be considered quite rude. While we consider the avoidance of eye contact to imply dishonesty, in other cultures it is used as a sign of respect. The watching of other people is another way in which eye contact can vary, with some cultures finding being observed as rude or threatening, while others finding it perfectly acceptable.

- *Posture*: Folded arms may come across as negative and defensive to us, but in other countries it is interpreted as being friendly and relaxed. Rules on posture can vary depending on gender in some countries, so if you are a woman, for example, be aware that sitting with your legs apart may be frowned on in some countries. As with all body language, our body posture may be interpreted as more positive or negative than we would expect depending on the culture norms we are dealing with. Do not be surprised if you are described as being quite reserved or hostile when you thought you were being friendly. You need to observe the posture of others and try and compensate as soon as possible without being too obvious.

- *Touch*: The amount and type of touching that is acceptable or expected will vary between cultures. Some cultures use touch only when in close relationships, such as within the family or with close friends. They may also touch when greeting, for example, when shaking hands. Other cultures consider touch to be friendly and will frequently use touch when interacting with others. The rules of touch can vary according to gender – in some cultures it may be acceptable for people of the same but not the opposite sex to touch, while in other cultures it maybe perfectly acceptable to touch people of either sex. The difference in attitudes and cultures may lead to people that rarely use touch to appear cold and distant to those who use touch frequently, who in turn will come across as pushy and disturbing to the former.

If touch is used when it is unacceptable to the other person, it can feel like an invasion of their privacy, and can cause concern and embarrassment. Touching someone inappropriately can have serious consequences, so it is best either to find out what is acceptable beforehand, be guided by their behaviour or avoid touching altogether.

Putting non-verbal communication into practice

The study of non-verbal communication is an area that has become very popular and grown rapidly over the last few years. It is becoming an important skill for anyone whose role involves interpersonal communication. Person specifications that are used to assess people when recruiting will now often have criteria that relate to non-verbal communication. This is an area that any up-and-coming supervisor needs to develop if they hope to gain their first managerial role and be successful thereafter.

Learning any new skill is difficult and will take time, patience and practice. It is unrealistic to expect to develop new skills in a short space of time. In fact, as with most learning in life, your development should be continuous as you become more aware of non-verbal communication in yourself and others as you experience different situations in life.

One of the difficulties with trying to read other people's body language is that they will try to hide their thoughts and feelings out of social politeness or for one of many other reasons. This can provide many conflicting messages, as people deliberately try to create a certain impression, so if we go for the obvious signals then we could easily make an incorrect assumption. We need to be alert as it may be the very subtle non-verbal clues that reveal their true intentions and you need to be highly observant to pick up on these very small details.

In addition, you need to keep an open mind, as people are individuals, each with different backgrounds and values and should be studied in an unbiased way. We do not all think and feel in the same way, so we cannot interpret other people from our own point of view alone. You will especially need to consider these differences if observing people from different cultures, as body language can vary significantly to the point of misunderstanding or offence.

If you feel uncomfortable with developing your own body language skills, as you feel that this is being false or manipulative, remember that you already display some of the learned signals that cover how you really feel. Every day we smile and say hello to people, no matter how sad or unwell we are feeling at the time. It is about ensuring the way you behave is acceptable in the world of business. Developing these skills is about helping you to understand others better and to ensure that you are communicating in the most effective way possible.

The way you currently use non-verbal behaviour has mostly been learned and is a matter of habit. Over time, these behaviours can be unlearned and replaced by more appropriate ones. If you have the opportunity, it is worth trying out any desired changes using role play. These are practical skills which are best learned and developed through practice, and it is better to do this in a safe environment, than at an important business function. The other advantage is that under these circumstances you can obtain feedback from an observer as you may be unaware of some of your own mannerisms. If you can video record yourself in action, then even better, as you will be able to clearly judge your performance for yourself, however excruciating at first!

In the end, it is a good idea to have a plan that you can use to develop the way in which you present yourself. How others perceive you is important to your success. This area should be constantly developed as the demand on your interpersonal skills will increase as your career progresses.

Being aware of how others interpret you and how you can interpret others will increase the effectiveness of your communication skills and reduce the chance of misunderstandings. In many situations, it all comes down to the image you portray, rather than any knowledge and technical skills, so make sure you give yourself the best chance at success.

Using body language to advantage is nothing new; in 'The Journal of a Modern Lady', Jonathan Swift wrote:

> Nor do they trust their tongue alone,
> But speak a language of their own;
> Can read a nod, a shrug, a look,
> Far better than a printed book;
> Convey a libel in a frown,
> And wink a reputation down. (Swift, 1729)

However, it is only in the last few decades that the study and use of body language has gained popularity in the business world and become a 'must have' if you are to succeed. Make sure that you make the most of all the opportunities available by working on your non-verbal communication skills constantly and make sure that you are aware of the image you portray at all times, not just when you think it matters. In this way, good use of body language will become more comfortable, rather than an 'add on', and it will be seen as more natural to others.

Further reading

Argyle, M. (1979) *Person to Person: Ways of Communicating*. New York: Harper & Row.

Hargie, O. D. W. (1996) *Handbook of Communication Skills*. Oxford: Routledge.

James, J. (2001) *Body Talk at Work*. London: Piatkus.

Pease, A. (1992) *Body Language: How to Read Others' Thoughts by Their Gestures*. London: Sheldon Press.

Pease, A. and Pease, B. (2004) *The Definitive Book of Body Language*. London: Orion.

Wainright, G. R. (2003) *Teach Yourself Body Language*. London: Hodder Education.

Index

Printed in the United Kingdom
by Lightning Source UK Ltd.
109749UKS00001BB/2

9 781843 342151